Weddings

First published in Great Britain in 1996 by
BROCKHAMPTON PRESS
20 Bloomsbury Street, London WC1B 3QA
a member of the Hodder Headline Group

This series of little gift books was made by Frances Banfield, Andrea P.A. Belloli, Polly Boyd,
Kate Brown, Stefano Carantino, Laurel Clark, Penny Clarke, Clive Collins, Jack Cooper, Melanie Cumming,
Nick Diggory, John Dunne, Deborah Gill, David Goodman, Paul Gregory, Douglas Hall, Lucinda Hawksley,
Maureen Hill, Dennis Hovell, Dicky Howett, Nick Hutchison, Douglas Ingram, Helen Johnson, C.M. Lee,
Simon London, Irene Lyford, John Maxwell, Patrick McCreeth, Morse Modaberi, Tara Neill, Sonya Newland,
Anne Newman, Grant Oliver, Ian Powling, Terry Price, Michelle Rogers, Mike Seabrook,
Nigel Soper, Karen Sullivan and Nick Wells.

ISBN 1 86019 4753
A copy of the CIP data is available from the British Library upon request.

Produced for Brockhampton Press by Flame Tree Publishing,
a part of The Foundry Creative Media Company Limited,
The Long House, Antrobus Road, Chiswick W4 5HY.

Printed and bound in Italy by L.E.G.O. Spa.

CELEBRATION

Weddings

Selected by Karen Sullivan

BROCKHAMPTON PRESS

Happy is the bride
the sun shines on.

Proverb

One wedding,
the proverb says,
begets another.

John Gay, *Wife of Bath*

In marriage there are no manners to keep up, and beneath the wildest
accusations no real criticism. Each is familiar with that ancient child
in the other who may erupt again… We are not ridiculous to ourselves.
We are ageless. That is the luxury of the wedding ring.

Enid Bagnold

Marriage is an act of will that signifies and involves a mutual gift,
which unites the spouses and binds them to their eventual souls, with
whom they make up a sole family – a domestic church.

Pope John Paul II

A successful marriage is an edifice that must be rebuilt every day.

André Maurois

It is obvious that all sense has gone out of modern marriage: which is, however, no objection to marriage but to modernity.

Friedrich Nietzsche

Chains do not hold a marriage together. It is threads, hundreds of tiny threads which sew people together through the years. That is what makes a marriage last – more than passion or even sex!

Simone Signoret

Marriage is popular because it combines the maximum of temptation with the maximum of opportunity.

George Bernard Shaw

A little weeping, a little wheedling, a little self-degradation, a little careful use of our advantages, and then some man will say – 'Come, be my wife!' With good looks and youth marriage is easy to attain. There are men enough; but a woman who has sold herself, even for a ring and a new name, need hold her skirt aside for no creature in the street. They both earn their bread in one way. Marriage for love is the beautifullest external symbol of the union of souls; marriage without it is the uncleanliest traffic that defiles the world.

Olive Schreiner

Like everything which is
not the involuntary result
of fleeting emotion but
the creation of time and
will, any marriage, happy
or unhappy, is infinitely
more interesting than
any romance, however
passionate.

W. H. Auden

A bride at her second
marriage does not wear
a veil. She wants to see
what she is getting.

Helen Rowland

Wherefore they are no more twain, but one flesh. What therefore God hath joined together, let not man put asunder.

Matthew, XIX: 6

He took the bride about the neck
And kissed her lips with such a clamorous smack
That at the parting all the church did echo.

William Shakespeare, *The Taming of the Shrew*

The problem with marriage is that it ends every night after making love, and it must be rebuilt every morning before breakfast.

Gabriel García Márquez, *Love in the Time of Cholera*

Algernon [speaking very rapidly]: Cecily, ever since I first looked upon your wonderful and incomparable beauty, I have dared to love you wildly, passionately, devotedly, hopelessly.

Cecily: I don't think that you should tell me that you love me wildly, passionately, devotedly, hopelessly. Hopelessly doesn't seem to make much sense, does it?

Algernon: Cecily!… I don't care for anybody in the whole world but you. I love you, Cecily. You will marry me, won't you?

Cecily: You silly boy! Of course. Why, we have been engaged for the last three months.

Algernon: For the last three months?

Cecily: Yes, it will be exactly three months on Thursday.

Algernon: But how did we become engaged?

Cecily: Well, ever since dear Uncle Jack first confessed to us that he had a younger brother who was very wicked and bad, you, of course, have formed the chief topic of conversation between myself and Miss Prism. And, of course, a man who is much talked about is always very attractive. One feels there must be something in him, after all. I dare say it was foolish of me, but I fell in love with you, Ernest.

Algernon: Darling. And when was the engagement actually settled?

Cecily: On the 14th of February last. Worn out by your entire ignorance of my existence, I determined to end the matter one way or other, and after a long struggle with myself I accepted you under this dear old tree here. The next day I bought this little ring in your name, and this is the little bangle with the true lovers' knot I promised you always to wear.

Oscar Wilde, *The Importance of Being Earnest*

All marriages are happy. It's the living together afterwards that causes all the trouble.

Raymond Hull

A happy marriage has in it all the pleasures of a friendship, all the enjoyments of sense and reason, and indeed, all the sweets of life.

Joseph Addison

If only the strength of the love that people feel when it is reciprocated could be as intense and obsessive as the love we feel when it is not; then marriages would be truly made in heaven.

Ben Elton, *Stark*

Wasn't marriage, like life, unstimulating and unprofitable and somewhat empty when too well ordered and protected and guarded? Wasn't it finer, more splendid, more nourishing, when it was, like life itself, a mixture of the sordid and the magnificent; of mud and stars; of earth and flowers; of love and hate and laughter and tears and ugliness and beauty and hurt?

Edna Ferber

A British mother's advice to her daughter on how to survive the wedding night: 'Close your eyes and think of England.'

Pierre Daninos

Deceive not thyself by over-expecting happiness in the married estate… Remember the nightingales which sing only some months in the spring, but commonly are silent when they have hatched their eggs, as if their mirth were turned into care for their young ones.

Thomas Fuller, *Of Marriage*

I have great hopes that we shall love each other all our lives as much as if we had never married at all.

Lord Byron

Music played at weddings always reminds me of the music played for soldiers before they go into battle.

Heinrich Heine

The reason husbands and wives do not understand each other is because they belong to different sexes.

Dorothy Dix

Marriage is not a word but a sentence.

Anonymous

Special Bridal Number

HOMES
AND GARDENS

The only solid and lasting peace between a man and his wife is doubtless a separation.

Lord Chesterfield

There is no more lovely, friendly, and charming relationship, communion or company than a good marriage.

Martin Luther

And if your hearts are bound together by love; if both are yielding and true, if both cultivate the spirit of meekness, forbearance, and kindness, you will be blessed in your home and in the journey of life.

Matthew Hale

A wedding day! A day
of rejoicing for two
families as well as for
the bride and groom.

Anonymous

Marriage is a great
institution, but I'm not
ready for an institution.

Mae West

The June roses over the porch were awake bright and early on that morning, rejoicing with all their hearts in the cloudless sunshine, like friendly little neighbours, as they were. Quite flushed with excitement were their ruddy faces, as they swung in the wind, whispering to one another what they had seen; for some peeped in at the dining-room windows, where the feast was spread, some climbed up to nod and smile at the sisters as they dressed the bride, others waved a welcome to those who came and went on various errands in garden, porch, and hall, and all, from the rosiest full-blown flower to the palest baby-bud, offered their tribute of beauty and fragrance to the gentle mistress who had loved and tended them so long.

Louisa May Alcott, *Good Wives*

Be cautious then, young ladies; be wary how you engage. Be shy of loving frankly; never tell all you feel, or (a better way still) feel very little. See the consequences of being prematurely honest and confiding and mistrust yourselves and everybody. Get yourselves married as they do in France, where the lawyers are the bridesmaids and confidants. At any rate, never have any feelings which may make you uncomfortable, or make any promises which you cannot at any required moment command and withdraw. That is the way to get on, and be respected, and have a virtuous character in Vanity Fair.

William Makepeace Thackeray, *Vanity Fair*

At American weddings, the
quality of the food is inversely
proportional to the social position
of the bride and groom.

Calvin Trillin

If you want to read about love
and marriage, you've got to buy
two separate books.

Alan King

I feel sad when I don't see you. Be married, why won't you? And come to live with me. I will make you as happy as I can. You shall not be obliged to work hard; and when you are tired, you may lie in my lap and I will sing you to rest… I will play you a tune upon the violin as often as you ask, and as well as I can; and leave off smoking if you say so… I would always be very kind to you, I think, because I love you so well. I will not make you bring in wood and water, or feed the pig, or milk the cow, or go to the neighbours to borrow milk. Will you be married?

Letter from an American suitor

My son is my son till he gets him a wife,
But my daughter's my daughter all of her life.

Proverb

No. 4384.—Volume 162.   The Illustrated London News, April 28, 1923.

PRICE TWO SHILLINGS.

THE ILLUSTRATED LONDON NEWS

LADY ELIZABETH BOWES-LYON.   H.R.H. THE DUKE OF YORK.

WEDDING NUMBER

PRICE TWO SHILLINGS; BY INLAND POST, 2/2½.   PUBLISHING OFFICE, 172, STRAND, LONDON, W.C.2.

It was so cold I almost got married.

Shelley Winters

A happy bridesmaid makes a happy bride.

Alfred, Lord Tennyson, *The Bridesmaid*

Wedding: a ceremony at which two persons undertake to
become one, one undertakes to become nothing, and
nothing undertakes to become supportable.

Ambrose Bierce, *The Devil's Dictionary*

Let there be spaces in your togetherness.

Kahlil Gibran, *The Prophet*

Here's to matrimony, the high sea for which
no compass has yet been invented.

Heinrich Heine

Let endless peace your steadfast hearts accord
And blessed plenty wait upon your board.
Let your bed with pleasures chaste abound
That fruitful issue may to you afford
Which may your foes confound;
And make your joys redound upon your bridal day, which is not long.

Edmund Spenser

It was because I felt and knew this, that I resolved to marry you. To tell me that I had already a wife is empty mockery: you know now that I had but a hideous demon. I was wrong to attempt to deceive you… I should have appealed to your nobleness and magnanimity at first, as I do now – opened to you plainly my life of agony – described to you my hunger and thirst after a higher and worthier existence – shown to you, not my resolution (that word is weak), but my resistless bent to love faithfully and well, where I am faithfully and well loved in return. Then I should have asked you to accept my pledge of fidelity, and to give me yours: Jane – give it to me now.

Charlotte Brontë, *Jane Eyre*

A man in love is incomplete until he is married. Then he is finished.

Zsa Zsa Gabor

FOR THE TOILET OF THE BRIDE.

ON this very morn of morns, the brightest and happiest of her life, every bride longs to look her best, so that shimmering silks and misty lace shall be a fit setting for charm and beauty. So what more natural than that she should use the Vinolia Toilet Preparations in her all-important toilet?

There is delicately scented Soap to soothe the fair skin, Tooth Paste to give a sparkling whiteness to the teeth, and Powder and Cream to yield a perfect bloom to the radiant cheek.

Premier Vinolia Soap.
6½d. per tablet.
Bath size tablet, 11d.

Vinolia Talcum Powder (Royal Series).
In Wedgwood Design Tins, 1/- and 1/6.

Vinolia Cream (Royal Series).
In Boxes, 1/3, 2/3, and 4/6.

Vinolia Tooth Paste (Royal Series).
In Tubes, 7½d., and 1/3.

RV. 67.

VINOLIA *Toilet Requisites*

VINOLIA COMPANY LIMITED. LONDON

Printed by HUDSON & KEARNS, LIMITED, Hatfield Street Works, Stamford Street, S.E. 1, and Published by GEORGE NEWNES, LIMITED, 8-11, Southampton Street, Strand, London, W.C. 2.

'Tis more blessed to give than receive; for example, wedding presents.

H. L. Mencken

What with songs, feasting and carousing, Adrienne's wedding is a lovely wedding. Five meat courses, three sweets, and the tiered wedding cake surmounted by a trembling plaster rose.

Colette, *My Mother's House*

Any intelligent woman who reads the marriage contract and then goes into it, deserves all the consequences.

Isadora Duncan

 39

Marrying to increase love is like gaming to become rich; alas,
you only lose what little stock you had before.

William Wycherley

Marriage must be a relation either of sympathy or of conquest.

George Eliot

Honour, riches, marriage blessing,
Long continuance, and increasing,
Hourly joys be still upon you!
Juno sings her blessings on you.

William Shakespeare, *The Tempest*

A husband is what's left of a lover after the nerve has been extracted.

Helen Rowland

Your most beautiful bride who with garlands is crown'd
And kills with each glance as she treads on the ground,
Whose lightness and brightness doth shine in such splendour
That none but the stars
Are thought fit to attend her.

Thomas Jordan, *Let Us Drink and Be Merry*

Happily the sunshine fell more warmly than usual on the lilac tufts on the morning that Eppie was married, for her dress was a very light one. She had often thought, though with a feeling of renunciation, that the perfection of a wedding dress would be a white cotton, with the tiniest pink sprig at wide intervals; so that when Mrs Godfrey Cass begged to provide one, and asked Eppie to choose what it should be, previous meditation had enabled her to give a decided answer at once.

Seen at a little distance as she walked across the churchyard and down the village, she seemed to be attired in pure white, and her hair looked like the dash of gold on a lily. One hand was on her husband's arm and with the other she clasped the hand of her father Silas.

'You won't be giving me away, father,' she had said before they went to church, 'you'll only be taking Aaron to be a son to you.'

George Eliot, *Silas Marner*

A marriage is no amusement but a solemn act, and generally a sad one.

Queen Victoria

When two young people set out on the voyage of life in a splendid argosy apparently laden with everything that makes life worth living, the woman, if generous and large-hearted, generally says to herself, 'Why should I make my darling take up the grind of a working life? Surely he will always find plenty to do worth doing, without going to an office every day, or even, say, taking up farming, or some other kind of country work?' He, naturally, heartily agrees; and so the two start out, happy and confident, feeling sure that they will live happily ever after.

Mrs Belloc Lowndes, *With all Her Worldly Goods*

Till age, or grief, or sickness must
Marry my body to that dust
It so much loves.

Henry King, *Exequy on His Wife*

Why should a foolish marriage vow,
Which long ago was made,
Oblige us to each other now
When passion is decayed?
We loved, and we loved, as long as we could,
Till our love was loved out in us both;
But our marriage is dead when the pleasure is fled:
'Twas pleasure first made it an oath.

John Dryden, *Marriage-a-la-Mode*

When a girl marries she
exchanges the attentions
of many men for the
inattention of one.

Helen Rowland

I am yours forever
And our co-equal
love
Will make the stars
to laugh with joy.

Christina Walsh

Meg looked very like a rose herself; for all that was best and sweetest in heart and soul, seemed to bloom into her face that day, making it fair and tender, with a charm more beautiful than beauty. Neither silk, lace, nor orange flowers would she have. 'I don't want to look strange or fixed up, today,' she said, 'I don't want a fashionable wedding, but only those about me whom I love and to them I wish to look and be my familiar self.'

Louisa May Alcott, *Good Wives*

The most happy marriage I can imagine to myself would be the union of a deaf man to a blind woman.

Samuel Taylor Coleridge

I've often wished to have a friend
With whom my choicest hours to spend,
To whom I safely may impart
Each wish and weakness of my heart.
Who would in every sorrow cheer,
And mingle with my grief a tear,
And to secure that bliss for life,
I'd like that friend to be my wife.

Victorian rhyme

The trouble with some women is that they get all excited about
nothing – and then marry him!

Cher

Marriage that does the hearts and wills unite
Is the best state of pleasure and delight.

Thomas Shadwell, *Epsom Wells*

To the best bride-bed will we,
Which by us shall blessed be;
And the issue there create
Ever shall be fortunate.

William Shakespeare, *A Midsummer-Night's Dream*

A man should marry someone like himself;
A man should pick an equal for a mate.

Geoffrey Chaucer, *'The Miller's Tale'*

A woman seldom asks
advice before she has
bought her wedding
clothes.

Joseph Addison, *The Spectator*

It is a truth universally
acknowledged, that a
single man in possession
of a good fortune, must
be in want of a wife.

Jane Austen, *Pride and Prejudice*

Marriage is nothing but a civil contract.

John Selden, *Table Talk*

All dear Nature's children sweet
Lie 'fore bride and bridegroom's feet,
Blessing their senses.

John Fletcher and William Shakespeare, *Two Noble Kinsmen*

If I were a King what would I do?
I'd make you a queen, for I'd marry you.

Victorian rhyme

Charlie Chaplin's HOME

HOME CHAT

2ᵈ

Wedding Number

Vol. CXL. No. 1819.
FEBRUARY 1st, 1930.

Love is moral even without legal marriage, but marriage
is immoral without love.

Ellen Key

Better wed over the mixen than over the moor.

Proverb

Marriage may be compared to a cage: the birds outside despair to
get in and those within despair to get out.

Michel de Montaigne, *Essays*

If you keep marrying as I do, you learn everybody's hobby.

Joan Fontaine

Honesty has ruined more marriages than infidelity.

Charles McCabe

Come let's be a comfortable couple and take care of each other! How glad we shall be, that we have somebody we are fond of always, to talk to, and sit with. Let's be a comfortable couple. Now do, my dear!

Charles Dickens

The amorous bird of night,
Sing spousal, and bid haste the evening star
On his hilltop, to light the bridal lamp.

John Milton, *'Paradise Lost'*

A bonny blue sky,
Tae welcome the bride,
As she gangs tae the kirk,
With the sun on her side.

Anonymous, *West Wind*

Tomorrow is our wedding day,
And we will then repair
Unto the Bell at Edmonton
All in a chaise and pair.

William Cowper, *'John Gilpin'*

Marriage is the only
war in which you sleep
with the enemy.

Anonymous

Men are April when they woo, December when they wed:
maids are May when they are maids but the sky
changes when they are wives.

William Shakespeare, *As You Like It*

Halloa! Here's a church!... Let's go in!... Here's Miss Skiffins!
Let's have a wedding!

Charles Dickens, *Great Expectations*

The sealing day betwixt my love and me,
For everlasting bond of fellowship.

William Shakespeare, *A Midsummer-Night's Dream*

The LADIES' FIELD

ROYAL WEDDING NUMBER

MARCH 4th, 1922.

PRICE TWO SHILLINGS.

VOL. XCVI. No. 1251.

Registered at the G.P.O.
as a Newspaper, and for
Canadian Magazine Post.

Entered as second-class
Matter at the New York,
N.Y., Post Office, 1903.

I will wed thee in another key,
With pomp, with triumph and with reveling.

William Shakespeare, *A Midsummer-Night's Dream*

Hail wedded love… sole propriety
In Paradise of all things common else.

John Milton, *'Paradise Lost'*

If it were not for the presents, an elopement would be preferable.

George Ade, *Forty Modern Fables*

Let me not to the marriage of true minds
Admit impediments. Love is not love
Which alters when it alteration finds,
Or bends with the remover to remove:
Oh, no! it is an ever-fixed mark.
That looks on tempests and is never shaken;
It is the star to every wand'ring bark,
Whose worth's unknown, although his height be taken.
Love's not Time's fool, though rosy lips and cheeks
Within his bending sickle's compass come;
Love alters not with his brief hours and weeks,
But bears it out even to the edge of doom.
If this be error and upon me proved,
I never writ, nor no man ever loved.

William Shakespeare, *'Sonnet'*

Wife and servant are the same,
But only differ in the name:
For when that fatal knot is tied,
Which nothing, nothing can divide:
When she the word obey has said,
And man by law supreme has made,
Then all that's kind is laid aside,
And nothing left but state and pride.

Lady Mary Chudleigh, *To the Ladies*

O come ye here to fight, young lord,
Or come ye here to play?
Or come ye here to drink good wine
Upon the weddin'-day.

Anonymous, *Katharine Johnston*

 73

When I see that profile of hers, I feel the only thing worth doing in the world is to grab her and start shouting for clergymen and bridesmaids to come running...

P. G. Wodehouse, *Plum Pie*

I was married by a judge. I should have asked for a jury.

George Burns

Wedlock – the deep, deep peace of the double bed after the hurly burly of the chaise-longue.

Ralph G. Martin, *Jennie*

No. 5038—Volume 187

The Illustrated London News
November 9, 1935.

THE ILLUSTRATED LONDON NEWS

WEDDING NUMBER

AMO

PRICE ONE SHILLING; BY INLAND POST, 1/2
Canada and Newfoundland, 1¼d.; Foreign, 2d.

PRINTED IN GREAT BRITAIN AND REGISTERED AS A NEWSPAPER FOR TRANSMISSION IN
THE UNITED KINGDOM AND TO CANADA AND NEWFOUNDLAND BY MAGAZINE POST.

PUBLISHING OFFICE: 346, STRAND,
LONDON, W.C.2.

When two people are under the influence of the most violent, most insane, most delusive, and most transient of passions, they are required to swear that they will remain in that excited, abnormal and exhausting condition until death do them part.

George Bernard Shaw, *Getting Married*

Nothing so surely introduces a sour note into a wedding ceremony as the abrupt disappearance of the groom in a cloud of dust.

P. G. Wodehouse, *A Pelican at Blandings*

Bride. A woman with a fine prospect of happiness behind her.

Ambrose Bierce

Dear Mrs A
Hooray Hooray
At last you are deflowered.
On this as every other day,
I love you. Noel Coward.

Noel Coward,
Wedding telegram to Gertrude Lawrence

I must dance bare-foot on her
wedding day.

William Shakespeare,
The Taming of the Shrew

A princely marriage is the brilliant edition of a universal fact, and, as such, it rivets mankind.

Walter Bagehot

There were some merry hymns and as soon as Ethel and Bernard were one the clergyman began a sermon about Adam and Eve and the serpent.

Daisy Ashford, *The Young Visiters*

Girls usually have a papier mâché face on their wedding day.

Colette

…win me, woo me, wed me,
ah weary me.

James Joyce, *Finnegan's Wake*

If ever it occurs, you may bet
your bottom dollar there'll be no
mooning and spooning about it.
I mean to marry money. She'll
have a good fat account at the
bank or she won't do for me.

James Joyce, *Dubliners*

Notes on Illustrations

Page 1 *The Village Wedding* by Sir Luke Fildes (Christopher Wood Gallery, London). Courtesy of The Bridgeman Art Library; **Page 3** *The Seamstress* by Charles Baugniet (Victoria and Albert Museum, London). Courtesy of The Bridgeman Art Library; **Page 4** *The Happy Couple, Victorian Card* (Private Collection). Courtesy of The Bridgeman Art Library; **Page 7** *The Arranged Marriage* by Vasili Vladimirovits Pukirev (Tretjakoff-Galerie, Moscow). Courtesy of The Bridgeman Art Library; **Pages 8-9** *Fresh from the Altar* by Jessica Hayllar (Christie's, London). Courtesy of The Bridgeman Art Library; **Page 11** *The Arnolfini Marriage* by Jan van Eyck (National Gallery, London). Courtesy of The Bridgeman Art Library; **Page 14** *Lovers by a Gate.* Courtesy of the Laurel Clark Collection; **Page 16** *Gathering Flowers* by W. S. Coleman (Oscar and Peter Johnson Ltd., London). Courtesy of The Bridgeman Art Library; **Page 19** *Signing the Marriage Register* by James Charles (Bradford Art Galleries and Museums). Courtesy of The Bridgeman Art Library; **Page 20** *The Bridesmaid* by Philip Richard Morris (Christopher Wood Gallery, London). Courtesy of The Bridgeman Art Library; **Page 22** *Homes and Gardens.* Courtesy of The Laurel Clark Collection; **Pages 24-5** *Wells Cathedral* by John Buckler (Victoria and Albert Museum, London). Courtesy of The Bridgeman Art Library; **Pages 28-9** *None but the Brave Deserve the Fair,* from the *Pears Annual, 1915* by J. Shaw Compton (A & F Pears Ltd., London). Courtesy of The Bridgeman Art Library; **Page 31** *The Illustrated London News – Wedding Number.* Courtesy of The Laurel Clark Collection; **Page 32** *'Here Comes the Bride', The Wedding of George and Martha Washington* by Jean Leon Jerome Ferris (Private Collection). Courtesy of The Bridgeman Art Library; **Page 35** *The Wedding* by Albert Guillaume (Christopher Wood Gallery, London). Courtesy of The Bridgeman Art Library; **Page 37** *Buttercups* by Mrs Louisa Starr Canziani (Cheltenham Art Gallery and Museums, Gloucestershire). Courtesy of The Bridgeman Art Library; **Page 38** *Vinolia.* Courtesy of The Laurel Clark Collection; **Page 41** *Flower Arrangements.* Courtesy of The Laurel Clark Collection; **Page 42** *Till Death do us Part* by Edmund Blair Leighton (Forbes Magazine Collection; New York). Courtesy of The Bridgeman Art Library; **Page 47** *Royal Wedding.* Courtesy of The Laurel Clark Collection; **Pages 48-9** *Changing Homes* by George Elgar Hicks (Geffrye Museum, London). Courtesy of The Bridgeman Art Library; **Page 50** *The Passing of The Fairy King and Queen.* Courtesy of The Laurel Clark Collection; **Page 53** *John Bull.* Courtesy of The Laurel Clark Collection; **Page 54** *The Bride* by Henri Lafon (Musée Carnavalet, Paris). Courtesy of The Bridgeman Art Library; **Pages 56-7** *The Wedding at the Photographer's* by Pascal Dagnan-Bouveret (Musée des Beaux-Arts, Lyons). Courtesy of The Bridgeman Art Library; **Page 59** *Home Chat – Wedding Number.* Courtesy of The Laurel Clark Collection; **Pages 62-3** *Health to the Bride* by Walter Dendy Sadler (Stapleton

Collection). Courtesy of The Bridgeman Art Library; **Page 64** *Illustrated London News.* Courtesy of The Laurel Clark Collection; **Page 67** *The Wedding Dress* by Frederick Daniel Hardy (Oldham Art Gallery, Lancashire). Courtesy of The Bridgeman Art Library; **Page 69** *The Wedding Reception* by Jean Beraud (Collection J. Kugel, Paris). Courtesy of The Bridgeman Art Library; **Page 70** *Ladies' Field – Royal Wedding Number.* Courtesy of The Laurel Clark Collection; **Page 75** *The Bride* by Konrad Beckermann (Josef Mensing Gallery, Hamm-Rhynern). Courtesy of The Bridgeman Art Library; **Page 76** *Illustrated London News – Wedding Number.* Courtesy of The Laurel Clark Collection; **Page 78** *The Wedding, Early Twentieth Century American Postcard* (Private Collection). Courtesy of The Bridgeman Art Library; **Page 81** *The Wedding Dress* by George Goodwin Kilburne (Phillips, The International Fine Art Auctioneers). Courtesy of The Bridgeman Art Library; **Page 82** *Signing the Register* by Edmund Blair Leighton (City of Bristol Museum and Art Gallery). Courtesy of The Bridgeman Art Library.

Acknowledgements: The Publishers wish to thank everyone who gave permission to reproduce the quotes in this book. Every effort has been made to contact the copyright holders, but in the event that an oversight has occurred, the publishers would be delighted to rectify any omissions in future editions of this book. W. H. Auden, from *Collected Shorter Poems,* reprinted courtesy of Faber & Faber Limited; *Stark* by Ben Elton © Ben Elton, 1989, reprinted courtesy of Sphere Books, a part of the Penguin Group; P. G. Wodehouse extracts © P. G. Wodehouse, reprinted courtesy of Herbert Jenkins and Penguin Books; Letter from an American Suitor, from *The Penhaligon Book of Love,* selected and edited by Sheila Pickles, 1988; Thomas Hardy reprinted courtesy of Penguin Books; *Good News Study Bible,* published by Thomas Nelson, 1986, extracts reprinted with their kind permission; *Penguin Book of Japanese Verse,* translated by Geoffrey Bownas and Anthony Thwaite, published by Penguin 1964, and reprinted with their permission.